THE
BABY WITCH'S
JOURNAL

THE BABY WITCH'S JOURNAL

Text by Anna Martin

An Hachette UK Company
www.hachette.co.uk

Summersdale Publishers Ltd
Part of Octopus Publishing Group Limited
Carmelite House
50 Victoria Embankment
LONDON
EC4Y 0DZ
UK

www.summersdale.com

Printed and bound in China

ISBN: 978-1-80007-714-0

THE
BABY WITCH'S
JOURNAL

A Spell Book for
New Witches

ASTRID CARVEL

summersdale

Contents

Why be
normal

when you can be magical?

NIKITA GILL

WELCOME, BABY WITCHES!

Let's start by getting one thing straight – a baby witch is simply a beginner witch; an acolyte or novice. You can be a baby witch at any time of life, and the witch community is one of the most welcoming and inclusive you can find. So, step out of the broom closet and start making magick!

It's an exciting time to be a baby witch as witches are everywhere – on social media and in some of the most talked-about television series and literature. But there's more to it than being on trend; it's a lifestyle choice, and one that can have a positive effect on every aspect of your life. Many people are turning to witchcraft as their spiritual path for self-care and a more joyful and meaningful existence. Witchcraft is individual and personal – it can be something as simple as performing a mindfulness ritual to give yourself courage for an important meeting, brewing a herbal remedy to ease a mild ailment, or creating a witch's ladder to manifest a long-held dream.

The Baby Witch's Journal will be your guide as you explore the different aspects of witchcraft so you can develop your natural aptitude and affinity for the craft. There are many types of witch and although this book doesn't provide an exhaustive guide to those types from which to choose, it will give you a clear indication of the path that best suits you. There are spells and rituals to try, ideas for forming a coven and finding like-minded souls, and a grimoire section to fill in the details of the spells that you have tried so you can record the outcomes and hone your craft.

Good luck, baby witch. Enjoy this magickal journey!

Magic or magick?

The word "magick" was coined by English occultist Aleister Crowley in the twentieth century to differentiate white magick from the magic of stage magicians. Magick with a "k" is about aligning with the forces of nature to manifest your aims rather than supernatural showmanship.

WHAT MAGICK CAN DO FOR YOU

Performing spells and rituals can enhance your life in so many wonderful ways. The skills that you will learn within these pages will be ones for life that you can revisit whenever you need inspiration, focus, strength, foresight or just an extra dose of luck. You don't need to join a coven, although hanging out with fellow witches can be great fun, and you don't need to practise regularly or pass a test to do it well. All you need is to believe.

The spells can be adapted, so, for example, if you don't have a particular colour candle or type of crystal, you can use whatever you have to hand as these items are simply setting the scene and helping you to focus. Being a witch needn't cost a thing; some of the most potent and powerful spells happen when the moon is in a certain phase or you have found a hag stone on the beach (a stone with a hole in it) to cast a spell, or a beautiful leaf or feather and incorporated it into your spell.

A word of warning

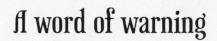

While Sabrina might be able to magic up a spell to banish monsters and save her friends, it's important to be aware of the limitations and dangers of witchcraft in the real world.

Most witches believe in the karmic law, which means that the craft should never be used for evil purposes. The karmic law states that what is sent out will return to you threefold, which means the bad luck you cast will be three times worse for you when it comes back – so think very carefully before you hex your ex!

Which Witch Are You?

Take the quiz to find out!

Which natural energy do you feel most connected to?

a) moonlight

b) rocks and crystals

c) water

d) the wisdom of trees

e) the healing power of herbs

Which animal would be your familiar?

a) hare

b) horse

c) raven

d) bear

e) cat

Where would you most like to cast your spells?

a) in a clearing, under a full moon

b) in a crystal cave

c) on a clifftop, during a storm

d) deep in the forest

e) at a kitchen table

What form of witchcraft fascinates you the most?

a) astrology

b) tarot and palmistry

c) working with the elements

d) manifestation

e) spell work

Which colour speaks to your aura?

a) indigo, like the midnight sky

b) purple, like a crystal ball

c) dark grey, like a stormy sea

d) white, like mist in a forest

e) pale green, like sunlight through leaves

Choose an accessory.

a) a telescope

b) a handheld mirror

c) a broomstick

d) a wicker basket

e) a cauldron

Where is your favourite place to hang out?

a) in the mountains

b) at ancient sites or in old cities

c) by the ocean

d) in the forest

e) in the garden

What would you use for your grimoire (spellbook)?

a) a planetary alignment calendar

b) a smartphone, because the screen can double up as a scrying mirror

c) an almanac full of information about the seasons and weather

d) an upcycled notebook

e) an old cookbook that has been passed down through the generations

What would you most like to use in your spells?

a) candles

b) runes

c) water and salt

d) earth

e) essential oils

Mostly **a** = cosmic
Mostly **b** = divination
Mostly **c** = weather
Mostly **d** = earth
Mostly **e** = kitchen

The first time I called
myself a "Witch" was
the most magical
moment of my life.

MARGOT ADLER

Chapter One

COSMIC WITCH

What is a cosmic witch?

This otherworldly witch uses celestial and planetary energy in their practice. They may pray to the moon goddess for guidance or seek the ancient wisdom of the universe through astrology. They time their spells and rituals in accordance with the lunar calendar and planetary positions. Sometimes a cosmic witch may feel they are not of this earth, as though their ancient soul resided on a different planet.

Tools: water infused with moonlight for cleansing negative energies; star signs to determine compatibility with others; tarot cards for a new moon reading to forecast the coming month; candlelight to represent the nurturing, life-giving sun; wishing on shooting stars; and honouring the seasons with feasts and rituals.

COSMIC VIBES

YOU ARE MAGICK

A Full Moon Ritual
to Perform with Friends

Many witches charge up and cleanse their crystals and wands by the light of the full moon. This simple full moon ritual offers a chance to focus on ambitions and new ventures, or, if there is nothing specific that you are aiming for, a boost of positivity, which is always welcome! This ritual is nice to do with a group of like-minded friends.

Find a quiet outdoor space – perhaps a garden so that you are not going to be interrupted or overlooked. Begin by making a circle with string or yarn. It needs to be large enough for the group to sit comfortably around it. Tie the two ends of the circle together to make the thread continuous. Light a tea-light each inside the circle and place in a heatproof container with sides, such as a bowl or a hurricane lamp, so that the flames aren't easily snuffed out by a gust of wind.

Have a small piece of rose quartz in front of each person within the circle. Place short lengths of fabric beside each person. These could simply be oddments picked up from a haberdashers or a torn-up old T-shirt that's past its best. The person who called the ritual may open the circle with the following words:

Here tonight a circle spun
For enchanting spells to be done!

20

Then the same person picks up a length of fabric, ties it to the string circle and says what they would like to achieve or manifest before the next full moon. Going clockwise around the circle, the next person picks up a piece of fabric, ties it to the string circle and says something that they would like to happen or experience, and so on. Keep going around the circle until everyone has spoken. If there is nothing in particular that you wish to achieve, then you can give thanks for your blessings. When the hopes, wishes and blessings are all attached to the string, everyone must pick up the circle and say this moon blessing:

Full moon, bright moon, hear my plea,

Blessings come, return to me.

Focus on the flickering candles and feel the full moon's energy. Close the circle by holding hands, blowing out the candles and all saying, "So mote it be," a common Pagan phrase to sign off a spell or ritual meaning, "So may it be". Each person can take their piece of rose quartz and keep it with them until the next full moon when the ritual can be performed again.

Moon Phases and Spellcasting

The moon has always held a powerful spiritual significance for witches, and many witches cast their spells in accordance with the phases of the moon, as each phase has pertinence to different types of spell. A pocket diary will contain the moon's phases or you can find the information online.

New moon:
NEW BEGINNINGS

This is the perfect time to perform spells that herald new beginnings as the new moon represents positive change. Use the new moon's power for finding employment, new love or a new home. It's also a potent time for fertility spells.

Waxing moon:
GROWTH AND BLOOM

This is when the moon is growing each night until it becomes a full moon. This period is good for attraction spells – ones to grow your wealth, improve health and draw friends and lovers to your side.

Full moon:
FULL POWER

This is the most powerful time for magick, so use this period wisely for casting spells for protection, wealth, love and good health. Some witches experience heightened psychic ability during a full moon.

Waning moon:
REMOVAL AND LETTING GO

This is when the moon appears to recede each night in the sky. It's the ideal time for repulsion spells, for example, if you want to banish negative forces from your life, take control of a difficult situation or soothe a fractious or anxious loved one.

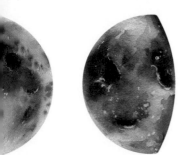   

Dark moon:
INTROSPECTIVE

This is when the moon appears to be invisible against the backdrop of the sun. This phase occurs three days prior to a new moon. Those who perform dark magick are particularly active at this time. Many white witches choose not to cast spells in this period, while others see it as a good time for spells that break negative cycles and bring justice to bear.

Lunar eclipses

This is another auspicious time to perform spells, especially when you bear in mind that a lunar eclipse only occurs during a full moon, so you are working with full-moon energy. Be particularly careful when performing spells during this time and choose your words and spells wisely.

There is no greater power
than that of the sun,
the moon, and a woman
who knows her worth.

NICOLE LYONS

Money luck full moon spell

This simple spell will help you manifest more cash. When performing the spells think carefully about how much money you need and what you will use it for.

You will need

- A green candle and holder
- A pin to carve into the candle
- A lighter

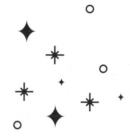

Method

Start by meditating on what you truly want and how much it is going to cost – think about how having the money will improve your life and visualize this new situation in as much detail as you can. When you have a clear mental image, think of one or two words that define what the item or experience is, such as "writing course" or "tattoo", and carve the word or words carefully into the side of the candle with your pin. It doesn't need to be neat (or legible!) as this is just for you and you're affirming your intentions.

Place the carved candle in a holder and light it. Meditate on the candle flame and think again about what you need the money for. Watch the candle burn down over the words that you have carved and then blow it out. When the candle stump has cooled, place it in your purse. The universe will respond by the next full moon.

FRESH START BUBBLE BATH

This one requires a little preparation to make the moon water, but it's worth it! The new moon is a good time to set new intentions, form healthy habits and start again – it's the celestial equivalent of a fresh coat of paint on your wall or a brand-new dress.

You will need

- A filled bubble bath
- A pink-coloured candle and holder
- A small bottle containing moon water

Method

First, make your moon water. To do this you will need a small container, preferably with a lip for decanting. Fill the container with tap water and place outside on a full moon night so the water can absorb the potent energies of the moon. When the morning comes, carefully pour the water into small airtight containers so they are ready to use for your spells – but be sure to use them before the next full moon.

On a new moon night, fill a bath with your favourite oils.

Place the pink candle in a holder beside the bath and light it – secure it in a safe spot where you're not going to knock it.

Now, submerge yourself in the warm water. Take some deep, calming breaths and pour the moon water into the bath. Swirl it with your hands and say:

Dear Sister Moon
I say goodbye to the bad and
*   welcome the good*
I deserve happiness
So mote it be!

Imagine the moon's healing energies swirling around you. Enjoy your bath and relax as the candle burns.

31

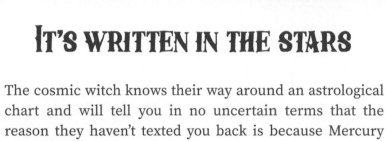

It's Written in the Stars

The cosmic witch knows their way around an astrological chart and will tell you in no uncertain terms that the reason they haven't texted you back is because Mercury has fiddled with their phone settings!

Astrology doesn't predict your future or define your personality; instead, it describes the potential for particular characteristics or events to come to light. Astrology can help you know what you are capable of as a human being, and when to take advantage of challenging or opportunistic times. It's important to remember that you are not controlled by the planets – but they can bring about certain atmospheres that can help or hinder you.

Your birth chart is a snapshot of the planets' exact positions at the time of your birth, which gives you a tremendous amount of insight into your personality. But the moment after that picture was taken the planets changed their positions. Astrologers describe these moving planets as "transiting" and their movements can provide information about your future.

Transits can highlight opportunities to be taken advantage of or challenges to be aware of. Most practised astrologers will be familiar with the planets' current positions but you can easily find out by looking up the current date in a book called a planetary ephemeris or discover this information online.

Zodiac elemental booster spell

We all have a zodiac sign that we were born under and with that comes an element that is associated with gifts and traits that pertain to your personality and appearance. These elements are earth, air, fire and water, and they are divided into the following zodiac signs – do you recognize yourself?

Fire signs
(Aries, Leo and Sagittarius)

ARIES   LEO   SAGITTARIUS

Fire attracts attention and is transformative. It gives fire signs charisma and the ability to change a mood or atmosphere.

Water signs
(Cancer, Scorpio and Pisces)

CANCER   SCORPIO   PISCES

Water is a precious life-giver with a magnetic, shifting quality. It gives water signs the gifts of intuition and sensitivity.

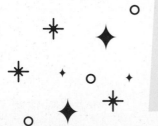
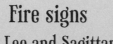

Air signs
(Gemini, Libra and Aquarius)

GEMINI

LIBRA

AQUARIUS

Air flows, expands and disperses. It gives air signs their ability to think creatively and make the impossible seem possible.

Earth signs
(Taurus, Virgo and Capricorn)

TAURUS

VIRGO

CAPRICORN

Earth is solid, reliable and anchoring. It gives earth signs the skills to build their dreams on firm foundations and make sensible decisions.

You can tune in to these gifts and harness these powers with a simple ritual. First, you need to work out which element you are influenced by in relation to your birth date – some are on the cusp so it may be that you are influenced by two elements (lucky you!).

You will need

Something that represents your element – this is a chance to get creative. For example, for an air sign you could use a feather or a paper plane; for a water sign you could use water from a tap or a raindrop-shaped pendant; for an earth sign you could have a small plant, a piece of pottery or a freshly picked flower; and for fire, a piece of forged metal such as silver jewellery or a matchbox.

Method

Go to a spot where you feel calm and where you're unlikely to be disturbed, such as a park, a quiet spot in the garden or a cosy nook in your home.

Relax your body by closing your eyes and taking in some deep breaths.

When you're feeling calm, take the item that represents your element(s) and meditate on it as you think of the qualities that you would like to enrich your life.

At heart we are all
powerful, beautiful,
and capable of
changing the world
with our bare hands.

DIANNE SYLVAN

Chapter Two

DIVINATION WITCH

What is a divination witch?

These witches have the precious gift of Second Sight. The ability to predict the future has been highly regarded for centuries; soothsayers and prophets – from the fifteenth-century soothsayer Mother Shipton to the sixteenth-century astrologer Nostradamus – have foretold wars, famine, humans on the moon and the rise and fall of dictatorships, among many other major events. But, these days, let's be honest, what we really want to know is what the lotto numbers are going to be on Saturday and where we will meet our soulmate, right?

TOOLS: a crystal ball or reflective surface for scrying and communing with spirits; a tarot deck to answer big and small questions about the future; loose-leaf tea to answer specific questions about the future; your palms for an overview of health, wealth and happiness; and your own intuition.

GIRL, YOU ARE DIVINE

✦ Open Your Third Eye ✦

Every person has the ability to open their third eye and use their sixth sense. It's a gift that we all have and, like a muscle, it needs to be used and worked on. Our third eye is our psychic or sixth sense that enables us to see what is hidden from our normal senses. While the third eye is invisible, it's thought to be located in the middle of the forehead, above the space between our eyebrows. It's also referred to as the pineal eye.

Visualization

During meditation, try picturing things in your mind's eye as if you were taking yourself on a mental journey. By visualizing, you are strengthening your third eye which will help you to see visions in the future.

Dream journalling

Often, visions will come to us through dreams, so it's key to keep a dream journal as you work on your third eye. If you have a vivid dream, write it all down the moment you wake so you won't forget it.

Aura readings

Clairvoyance isn't just about seeing into the future; you can also use it to read the auras around you. Go to a public place: a coffee shop, a bookstore or a park. Then, start looking at all the people walking by – do they have a certain colour around them? Write it down!

she
BELIEVED
she could
» ···· so ···· «
SHE DID

Reading Tea Leaves

The ancient art of tasseography is one of the best budget ways to foretell the future because all you need is a kettle, a teacup and some loose-leaf tea.

While waiting for the kettle to boil, heap a teaspoon of tea leaves into a teacup. Pour the water into the cup and wait for it to cool before enjoying your tea. While sipping your tea, contemplate a question about your future that you would like to know the answer to.

When there is a small amount of liquid left in the cup, hold the cup in your left hand and swirl the tea leaves from left to right three times. Carefully turn the cup over so that it's upside down on the saucer, rotate the cup three times clockwise and then turn the cup so it's back to being upright on the saucer.

The remaining tea leaves will have formed shapes in the cup by clustering together. These shapes will provide the answers that you seek! It might just look like blobs of tea leaves in the first instance, but tasseographers over the centuries have detected consistent patterns and discovered five main symbols: animals, fantastical beings, letters, numbers and objects.

When reading the leaves, you should look at the cup as if it were divided into four:

The rim represents the present.

The sides of the cup are the near future.

The bottom of the cup denotes the far future.

The handle represents the querent (the person who is having their fortune told).

There are over 150 symbols in the tasseographer's armoury, but these are some of the most common and what they represent:

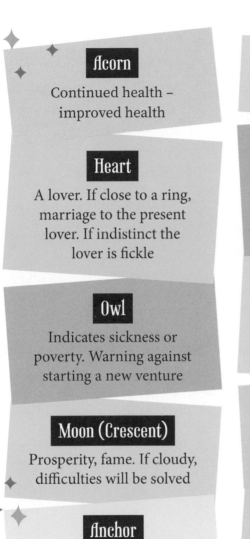

Acorn
Continued health – improved health

Heart
A lover. If close to a ring, marriage to the present lover. If indistinct the lover is fickle

Owl
Indicates sickness or poverty. Warning against starting a new venture

Moon (Crescent)
Prosperity, fame. If cloudy, difficulties will be solved

Anchor
Lucky symbol. Success in business or in love. If blurred or indistinct just the reverse

Triangle
Unexpected good fortune

Heavenly Bodies
(Sun, Moon, Star)
Good luck – great happiness and success

Palm Tree
Good omen, success in any undertaking. Single people learn of marriage

Elephant
Good luck – good health and happiness

Birds
Good luck. If flying, good news from the direction it comes. If at rest, a fortunate journey

FORTUNE TELLING WITH YOUR PHONE

Scrying is the ancient practice of gazing into or upon a smooth, translucent surface to see visions of the future or receive guidance. Images may appear in the form of words, pictures or symbols, which can be interpreted into prophecies and revelations – insights that only our third eye can see.

Black-mirror scrying (also referred to as catoptromancy) is the modern witch's way to scry. The black mirror refers to the screen on smartphones, tablets and TVs. If you wish to scry on the go, just pull out your smartphone and open your third eye.

Find a quiet place with minimal light and turn off your phone. Begin by giving the screen a good clean with a soft cloth. Then perform a mindful cleanse, imagining a pure whitelight encircling the screen.

Meditate and soften your gaze on the black mirror, allowing your clairvoyant abilities to surface, and watch and wait for images to appear – these could be physical images or ones in your mind's eye. Try to fix your gaze in one place. The mirror acts as a portal into your subconscious, bringing hidden visions to the surface. Scrying requires patience and it is a skill that develops over time – many witches report seeing wispy clouds or loose shapes on the black mirror, while others will experience more lucid thoughts – make sure you write down your experiences to allow time to decipher them. Spend around 15 minutes on this exercise.

Slowly bring your awareness back to your surroundings. Once you're back in the present, check your notes to decipher the messages. Some of these messages may not make sense to you so take a moment to consider them. For extra help, get a dream dictionary to look up the meanings of certain symbols.

Here are some common symbols and their meanings:

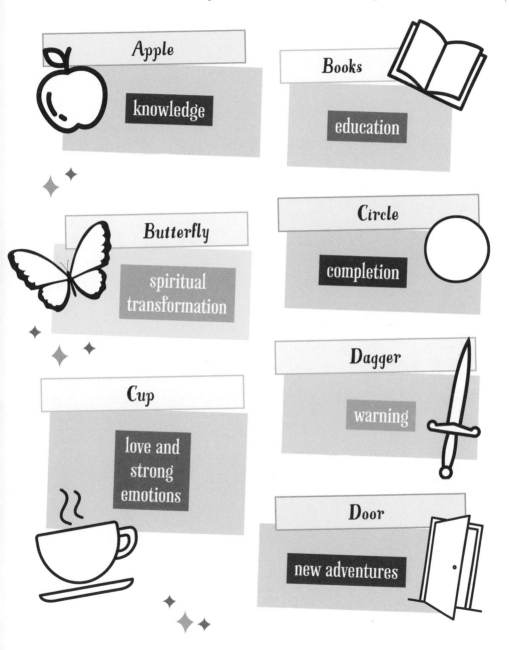

Apple — knowledge

Books — education

Butterfly — spiritual transformation

Circle — completion

Cup — love and strong emotions

Dagger — warning

Door — new adventures

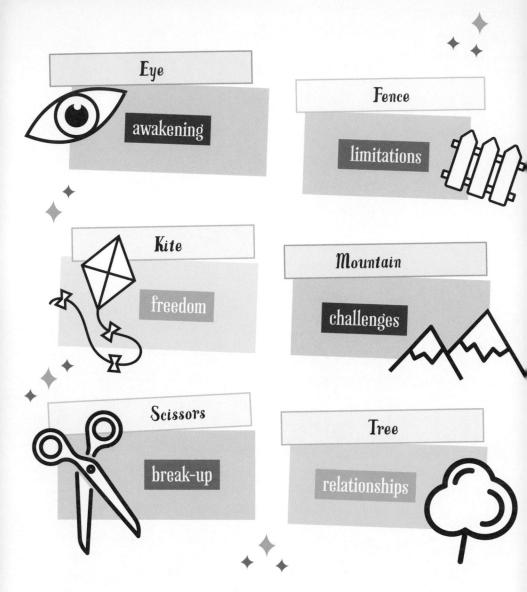

Eye — awakening

Fence — limitations

Kite — freedom

Mountain — challenges

Scissors — break-up

Tree — relationships

Seeing numbers, words or letters can evoke personal meaning for you in your own life.

Numbers usually mean length of time or quantity. Letters could mean someone's initials or a location. Words that have certain associations with you can also appear.

TALK TO THE HAND: PALMISTRY FOR BEGINNERS

Wouldn't it be great to look to your hands for guidance? Those lines on your palms all have a particular meaning and their placement can make all the difference. You can read both palms – the non-dominant hand reveals your potential and your future, while the dominant hand looks to your past. Start by looking at the palm on your dominant hand and familiarize yourself with the main lines on the illustration below – the head, life and heart lines.

The Life Line

This is the line that curves around the base of your thumb and indicates your character and the key events in your life. Here are a few things to look out for:

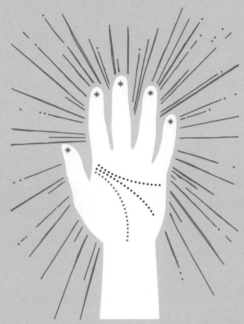

Broken line: struggles, loss, unexpected change.

Close to the thumb: chronic fatigue.

Curved line: high energy.

Deep line: smooth life path.

Faint line: low energy.

Forked line: interruption and redirection in life, scattered energies.

Long line: good health and stamina, vitality, well-balanced life.

No line: anxious person.

Short and deep: able to overcome physical problems with ease.

Short and faint: indecision.

The Head Line

Also known as the wisdom line, the head line appears above the life line and runs across the palm. Here are a few interpretations for this line:

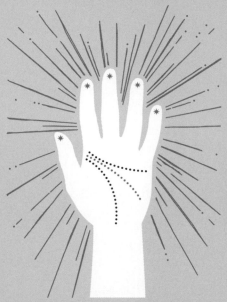

Chain (small loops that make up the line): you will have to make many difficult choices.

Crossed lines: emotional crisis in your life.

Curvy and faint: short attention span.

Deep and long: profound thinker.

Diagonal line: good at planning and self-expression.

Horizontal line: practical and down-to-earth.

Life line and head line are separated: lust for life.

Line crosses entire palm: self-centred, ambitious.

Short line: prefer physical adventures over intellectual ones.

Straight line with chains: realistic thinker.

The Heart Line

This line is located at the top of the palm and runs horizontally.
It covers your emotional life and relationships.
Here are some things to look out for:

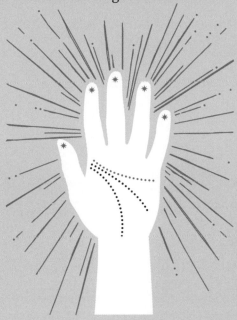

Curved line: many flings but not many serious relationships.

Line starts between index and middle fingers: you fall in and out of love easily.

Line starts under your index finger: you will have a happy and satisfied love life.

Line starts under your middle finger: you will be relentless in relationships.

Long line: you express emotions well.

Parallel with life line: practical in relationships.

Short line: little interest in relationships.

Straight line: you are romantic.

Touches the life line: heartbreak hits you hard.

The Health Line

There is no fixed starting point for the health line.
It can travel from the base of the little finger and go down
across the palm or it can begin just below the heart line and
connect with the life line. Here are some things to look out for:

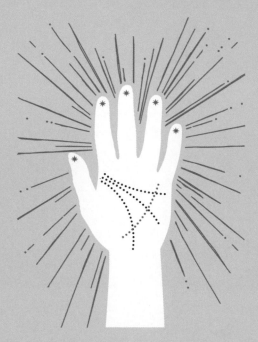

Bent in an arc: loss of strength.

Crossed by short lines: accident-prone.

No line: no health problems!

Short or made up of many lines: multiple health issues
throughout life.

Wavy line: potential issues with digestive tract, liver or gall
bladder.

There are more lines to look for, including:

The fate line represents how much of a person's life will be influenced by circumstances out of their control. It also represents how lucky you are. The fate line is a vertical crease in the centre of the palm, near the life, heart and head lines. The longer and deeper the line is, the more connected you are with destiny.

If you can see the letter "M" among the lines of your palm, it has a special meaning and is pretty rare. The M is formed when the three major lines are in alignment and are connected together by the fate line. The M is believed to be a blessing of good fortune. People with the M marking are creative, motivated and a great judge of character.

The marriage line reveals – you guessed it – your future marriages! Well, at least your romantic relationships if marriage isn't your thing. The marriage line is located on the side of your hand in a horizontal line or lines under your little finger. The marriage line can range from one line to three. More lines mean you'll get married or be in a serious relationship multiple times. Long lines mean longer relationships, while short lines mean shorter relationships. A marriage line that is curved upward can mean that a person will be single all their life or marry later.

The family lines are vertical lines under the little finger or between this finger and the ring finger. These lines represent how many children you will have in your lifetime. The family line/s can be isolated (having children outside of marriage or a relationship).

WAX SCRYING

A candle wax reading is a little like reading tea leaves: the premise is to use your intuition to decipher messages from shapes and patterns – in this case, those of wax drippings formed in water.

You will need

- A scrying bowl – this could be a simple shallow dish from your kitchen
- Water
- A candle
- A lighter
- A notepad and pen

Method

Fill your scrying bowl with clear water at room temperature. Moon water is best, but tap water is fine to use too.

Take some deep breaths to gain focus. When you are ready, visualize the question you would like to ask and then hold it in your mind.

Light your candle and hold it carefully over the water-filled scrying bowl with the wick tilted toward the water. This is so the wax can drip directly into the scrying bowl and not over your hand!

Hold your candle like this for a few moments, letting a few drips of wax fall into the water below. Concentrate on the candle's flame – you must give the wax and water time to blend before you look.

Blow out your candle and set it aside. You can now peer into your scrying dish.

The most important tool you have at your disposal is your intuition; there are certain patterns and shapes that will have a personal resonance only you will understand. However, there are some things you can look out for. For example, individual blobs of wax may resemble an object or an animal. Groups of identical formations could indicate numbers which might then indicate days, months or years. Letters could indicate someone's name.

These impressions may not make sense right away, so it can be helpful to make a note of your findings for future reference when other events have unfolded.

There are no right or wrong answers to the art of wax scrying. Keep practising, trust your intuitive self, and with experience you will understand what certain formations mean for you.

Chapter Three
WEATHER WITCH

What is a weather witch?

A *tempestarius* was a witch in medieval times who could manipulate the weather and summon squalls and tempests at will to make it treacherous for marauders to invade or ensure fine weather for crops. The modern weather witch is sensitive to the changing seasons and works with the elements for their craft. They love the drama of thunder and lightning and often like to create a storm in their spellcasting.

Tools: Think wild and free when it comes to the weather witch, such as driftwood, seaweed and pebbles from a beach walk; acorns and pine cones; a twig from a lightning-struck tree for a wand; rainwater collected on the full moon; salt-stained flotsam; or a raven's feather – anything that has absorbed the weather's unrivalled power.

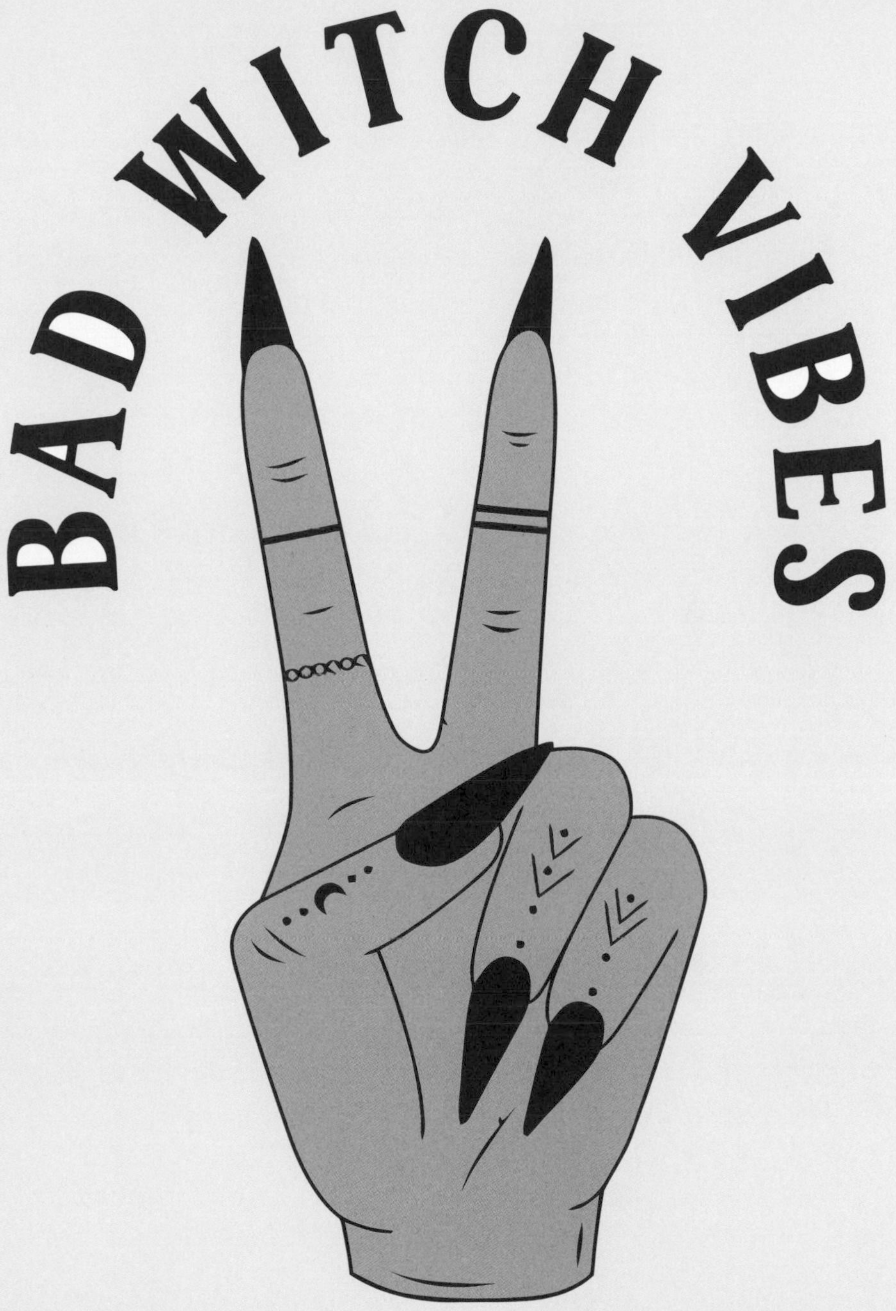
BAD WITCH VIBES

Summoning the Wind

Summoning the wind and asking to use its energy can boost the potency of any spell that you cast.

This ritual has been practised for hundreds of years and can be very personal. Some witches whistle to call the wind and can control its strength with the pitch and volume they use. Other witches ring a small bell.

The simplest way to call down the wind is to find a wide-open space, ideally a hilltop if you can, and speak these words aloud:

I summon the wind

The wind of desire

I summon the wind

The wind that will inspire!

Take a moment to enjoy the air against your face, whether that is a gentle breeze or a strong gust. Breathe deeply and visualize the energy of the wind coursing through you.

When it is time to cast your next spell, connect to this energy once again, remembering how the wind felt as it combed through your hair or the sound it made as it blew through the trees.

Listen to the wind,

It talks.

Listen to the silence,

It speaks.

Listen to your heart,

It knows.

NATIVE AMERICAN
PROVERB

Storm Bottle for Protection

Witch bottles have been used for centuries as protection against dark magick. Some early excavated examples include bottles containing needles, hair, herbs, feathers and tangled thread. These would have been buried in the hope of capturing harmful intentions and drawing them away from the intended recipient. If you feel as though you are under a spell or the victim of another witch's wrath, here's how to make your own storm bottle.

You will need

- A small glass bottle with a stopper that closes firmly
- Something that belongs to the person that requires protection, such as a lock of hair
- Some wool tied in knots – to entangle the bad spirits
- Salt or sand
- A few drops of seawater or moon water (see page 30)
- A black candle
- A lighter

Method

Put the lock of hair, wool, salt or sand and water into a bottle and think carefully about the bad feelings or intentions that you wish to banish. Say the following words:

With this bottle

I capture the storm unleashed on me

Return to sender

So mote it be!

Carefully light the black candle and drip the wax where the lid joins the bottle in order to seal it for eternity.

Now bury the bottle deep enough in a place where it will not be disturbed.

A WINTER WATER SPELL TO RE-ENERGIZE

The world outside may be frozen and still, but not all energies sleep! Snow and ice can play a key role in winter witchcraft.

Water can exist in all three states – a solid, a liquid and as a gas – which makes it a powerful and unique element. Snow is perhaps the most magical form water can take because it can reveal itself in different ways; it can be light and powdery, it can fall in feathery flakes or it can be heavy and wet. These different forms make snow the perfect ingredient for transformation and energy flow spells. If you feel that you have become stuck in one mindset, or if you simply need an energy boost, this spell can help you move into a more flexible space by increasing your energy flow.

All you need is a sacred vessel to collect a handful of snow – your favourite bowl or mug will do! To boost the potency of this spell, use your finger to inscribe words or draw a symbol into the snow. There is no right or wrong answer; simply choose something that has personal resonance for you.

Leave the bowl of snow in your bedroom. As you lie down to sleep, imagine the natural energy swirling around the snow as it melts overnight. Visualize the same energy swirling about your body as your own energy flow increases.

WISHING BUBBLES

No one grows out of a love for blowing bubbles! Here's a sweet spell to make a wish come true.

You will need

- Incense cone
- A cauldron or heatproof dish
- A bottle of bubble mixture and wand

Method

Begin by burning the incense in your cauldron or heatproof dish. Allow the scent to permeate the air and pass the bottle of bubbles over it a few times.

While doing so, concentrate on your wish and the ideal outcome – imagine it in as much detail as you can.

Take your mixture outside to a quiet spot and blow your bubbles. With each breath, imagine you are filling the bubbles with your wish.

Watch the bubbles fly off into the sky, full of your intentions – as they pop, the wish is released.

FIREWORKS EMPOWERMENT RITUAL

This ritual is for adding fuel to a dream or desire. It's a noisy ritual and must be done outdoors as it involves setting off fireworks.

Consider your dream when choosing the colour of your fireworks: if your dream revolves around wealth, then pick golds and greens; if the spell is for love, choose reds and pinks; for healing and purification, choose white.

The fireworks need to be left on an image of a pentacle for the days leading up to the full moon. On the night of the full moon, lay out the fireworks in your garden and as you do so, concentrate on your goal and visualize the outcome.

Light the fireworks – being careful to adhere to the safety instructions – and as they burst, light up the sky and rain down in their colours, the wish is released.

Manifesting with the Weather

If you are looking for a simple yet powerful technique to achieve your dreams and desires, then manifesting using the magick of the weather might be just the thing for you.

Although crystals and essential oils can help amplify your energy, you don't need any expensive equipment to manifest. In fact, the most valuable tool you can use is the magickal and natural (and free!) power of the skies:

 Sun

This works to manifest abundance and mental wellbeing. Feeling the warmth of the sunlight on your face is one of the most mood-boosting experiences the world has to offer. To manifest using sun energy, sit somewhere comfortable in the sun and close your eyes. An affirmation, visualization or just sitting with a sense of certainty that what you are manifesting is already yours is all it takes – it really is that simple!

 Rain

This works to manifest cleansing and healing. A sudden rain shower can be incredibly invigorating, and it is for this reason that rain is the perfect tool to manifest better health or to wash away sorrows. You don't need to be outside to manifest with the rain – simply sitting by a window with your eyes closed, listening to the patter of the raindrops against the glass is all you need.

✦ Snow ✦

This works to manifest energy and inspiration. There is nothing quite so magical as the sparkle of fresh snow and nothing quite so fun as making a snowman. As such, snowy weather is best used to manifest this wonderful sense of joy and energy into your life, long after the snow has melted. Let the refreshing chill course through you as you manifest.

✦ Wind ✦

This works to manifest strength and change. From a gentle breeze to a powerful hurricane, wind is one of the most changeable elements. Harnessing the power of the wind can bring positive change into your life, whether that is something specific like a new job, or simply something new and interesting. To manifest with the wind, all you need to do is pay attention to how the breeze feels through your hair, or to the sound of a storm howling outside your window.

Those who don't
believe in magic
will never find it.

ROALD DAHL

Chapter Four

EARTH WITCH

What is an earth witch?

Nature is spell-binding – and earth witches understand this. Happiest outside in the fresh air, they live in harmony with all living things. Earth witches learn from the earth and channel its natural energy in order to grow, bloom and flourish. Just as trees put down roots, earth witches' deep respect for and connection to nature means they are very grounded and powerful.

Tools: earth witches can make use of anything that has been born of the earth. This could include twigs for balance; rock salt for purification; windfall acorns for prosperity; and clay to make talismans.

How to Find Your Wand

When it comes to witchcraft, the most powerful tool at your disposal is your mind. It can be fun to use other items to enhance your spellcasting experience too, such as a cauldron or an altar. But the most magickal item in your witch's toolbelt would, of course, be a wand!

You don't need to spend money to find the perfect wand. Enjoying a forage in your local woods or park is the best way to ensure your wand is one of a kind.

Most witches believe in the karmic law. Therefore, it is important to harm no living thing – so don't go snapping something off the nearest tree! The best wood to use is a dried twig that has fallen to the ground. In fact, found objects tend to be the most powerful.

The right wand will find you, so see what catches your eye and use your intuition. Pay attention to the way the twig feels in your hand, noticing its texture and balance, for example.

Prepare your wand by removing any leaves and then store it somewhere indoors to dry out. You can remove the bark and smooth the wood as desired. Some witches carve symbols into the wood or add a crystal to the tip.

Make sure to give thanks to the earth for its gifts before you claim your wand.

Drawing down the moon

Before you can use your wand, you must purify and empower it by the light of a full moon. Stand outside with your wand on a full-moon night and point it at the moon to draw down its power. Other natural phenomena are also used to empower a wand. For example, leaving it out in a storm will boost your wand with fearlessness; leaving it in the rain will serve to cleanse and purify it; and pointing it toward a rainbow will encourage wish fulfilment.

Wand wood

Think about the types of spells that you wish to perform to help source the most suitable wood. Here are some examples of different woods and their special properties:

Apple
love and family

Ash
clairvoyance and good fortune

Beech
wisdom

Blackthorn
protection

Chestnut
balance

Cypress
for communicating with the dead

Hazel
healing and wisdom

Oak
strength

Rowan
clairvoyance and protection

Willow
healing

Nature wishes

This is a creative form of spellcasting and one of the nicest ways of performing a spell for another person. It takes time but the results – as long as the intentions are good – are worth it.

Wish bags traditionally contain one or more objects that can then be carried discreetly in a pocket or handbag.

Ingredients that can be used include small items significant to a spell, such as a feather, earth, seeds or pips – the options are infinite. The intention of the wish bag should be written clearly on a sheet of white paper and the items within the bag can be sprinkled with herbs or glitter.

The wish bags are often made from red felt, but any fabric can be used and it's up to you how elaborate you make it.

To charge your wish bag with magickal energy, place it next to a candle.

Light the candle and focus your energy on visualizing the outcome of the spell or imagine the obstacles falling away in order for you to reach your goal.

These spells can be performed over several days until the candle has burned down. You can then carry your wish bag around with you until the spell has worked.

Alternatively, if the wish bag is for a friend in need, give them the wish bag and candle. Instruct them to light the candle when they have a quiet moment and focus on their wish while holding the bag.

As before, the candle can be lit over several days until it has burned down. Encourage your friend to keep the wish bag with them, either on their desk or bedside table or in a pocket or handbag.

Ideas for natural finds to place in your wish bag:

Acorn

luck, prosperity and sexual potency

Clover

life, luck and abundance

Horn

repels the "evil eye" and is a symbol of nature, fertility and sexuality

Horseshoe

luck

Sycamore leaf

power and luck, a symbol of access to hidden things

Lightning-struck wood

protection against all harm

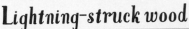

Pine cone

luck, favourable influences, protection from harm, repels bad intentions

Salt

purification, repels evil

Silver

protection and wealth

Smudge and Go!

Smudge sticks have been used for thousands of years to disperse bad energy. They are fairly simple to make – using fresh herbs bound with string – but they need to be prepared in advance and dried before use. If you don't have a smudge stick to hand, here's a "cheat's" version.

You will need

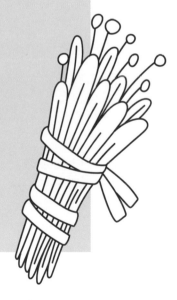

- A piece of parchment paper (approx. A4) that can be made into a small paper bag
- Gummed paper tape, or washi tape
- A handful of dried sage and sagebrush leaves
- A sprinkling of cloves
- Charcoal stick
- Twine
- Heatproof dish or cauldron in which items can be burned safely
- Matches

Method

Create a small bag out of the parchment paper and secure the edges with paper tape, leaving an opening.

Gather dried sage and sagebrush leaves, cloves and a small piece of charcoal stick and place them all into the bag.

Tie up the bag with twine and pop it in your heatproof dish or cauldron.

Light the smudge stick/bag and walk around the house to allow the incense to permeate all areas. Then open the front door and place the heatproof dish on the doorstep until the smudge stick has burned down to ash – leave it there until the following day.

Dispose of the ash around the roots of a fruit tree or potted plant. An example of negative energy could be someone gossiping about you. In this case, if you know their name, whisper it as you watch the burning embers.

Juniper
To reinvigorate
the mind and
energize the body

Mugwort
Enriches
your dreams
and cleanses
negative vibes

White Sage
For purification
and dispelling
negativity

Lavender
For tranquility,
calm and psychic
protection

Rosemary
For courage and
protection

Cedar
To boost luck in
a new home or
new relationship

Palo Santo
Encourages calm
and soothes a
troubled mind

A SPELL JAR
TO STAY GROUNDED

Immersing yourself in nature is the perfect way to help you keep your head during a stressful time. Bottling earthly agents and their energies can help bring your attention back to the natural world when you're not outside.

You will need

- A jar with a lid or stopper that closes firmly
- A selection of natural objects that come from something "alive", such as a fallen leaf, feather or acorn
- A pinch of soil
- A candle
- A lighter

Method

Take the jar along with you when you collect the natural objects. When you're ready, combine the elements and place them in a jar. Pay attention to your senses as you do so. Notice how the fresh air feels on your face and how your feet feel against the ground.

Stopper the bottle. Seal it with wax from the lit candle as soon as you get home to ensure that none of the natural energy escapes.

Whenever you feel you need grounding, take the bottle in your hand and connect to the energies within by recalling the sensations you felt outside.

Go on a witchy forage!

Found objects have a particular potency when spellcasting so keep your eyes open for natural objects that catch your eye. For example, sometimes the shape and smoothness of a stone can feel nice in your palm, or an autumn leaf in a fiery red sings against the dark earth and makes you want to pick it up, or a feather might float past you on the wind that you manage to catch. When items speak to you in such a way, gather them and save them for spells. However, be sure to thank the earth for its gifts before you take them.

Manifest Your Goals

Soil has the natural capacity to grow and nurture life itself. This incredible energy can be harnessed to boost your manifestation practice in this simple spell.

You will need

- A pen
- A slip of paper
- A seed and somewhere to plant it – a pot or garden

Method

Write your intention on a slip of paper, making sure to be as specific as possible to give the universe a clear message. Always write in the first person, using the present tense – and keep it positive! For example, "I am a wildly successful writer".

Bury your intention, along with a seed, in a pot or in your garden. Read your intention aloud as you do so.

Take good care of your little seedling, making sure that it gets plenty of water and sunlight. As your plant grows, the life-giving soil will contribute vital energy to your manifestation process.

A SIMPLE SPELL
TO REPLENISH YOUR ENERGY

Trees have always been closely associated with magick. They regenerate every spring, they sustain life in their branches, they tower above our heads and some may even stand for a thousand years. For these reasons, they are known for their strength, wisdom and talent for keeping secrets.

Sit with your back against a tree. A strong, older tree works best, but you can use your intuition to choose a tree that feels right for you.

Close your eyes and take some deep breaths. Feel the stability of the tree against your back. Note the texture of the bark and the sound of the breeze through its branches. Visualize the timeless energy flow of the tree, travelling up from the roots, through the trunk and finally nourishing the leaves. As you do so, imagine this same life-giving energy flowing into your body.

When you feel replenished, make sure to give thanks to the tree. You can return to nurture your bond whenever you choose.

Conchomancy

Seashells are the sort of thing you can't resist picking up on a beach walk. Here are the different types of common seashell and their magickal properties:

Clam

Protection • Balance
Love • Keeping secrets

Cockleshell

Friendship • Innocence
Childhood • Parenting

Cowrie

Feminity • Moon magick
Personal growth • Fertility

Limpet

Resilience • Endurance
Family ties • Strong bonds

Oyster

Beauty • Longevity
Individuality • Deep thinking

Razor clam

Fragility • Truth
Kindness • Hope

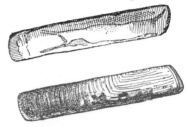

Scallop

Relationships • Healing
Resolving differences • Desire

Tower shell

Progress • Positivity
Confidence • Decision-making

Whelk

Success • Emotional strength
Change • Travel

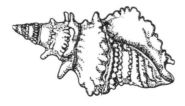

You can keep them as lucky talismans on your desk or by your bed and allow them to radiate their energy.

ᴴᴀɢ STONES

There are so many magickal things to be found along a beach, from beautiful shells and tumbled pebbles to driftwood and flotsam. But perhaps the most enchanting object hiding along the coastline is the hag stone.

Hag stones are ordinary stones with a hole running through them. They have enchanted us since ancient times and are believed to have magickal properties, from clairvoyance to warding off negative energy. This is because only good energy can pass through the hole or portal, whereas negativity is too large and inflexible.

Next time you find yourself by the ocean, keep a casual lookout for your very own hag stone. Remember, the hag stone will find you, you don't find the stone.

Uses of hag stones:

A doorway or window to keep out negative energies

Wear around your neck for protection

Peep through the hole for clairvoyance

Attach one to your keys and never lose them again!

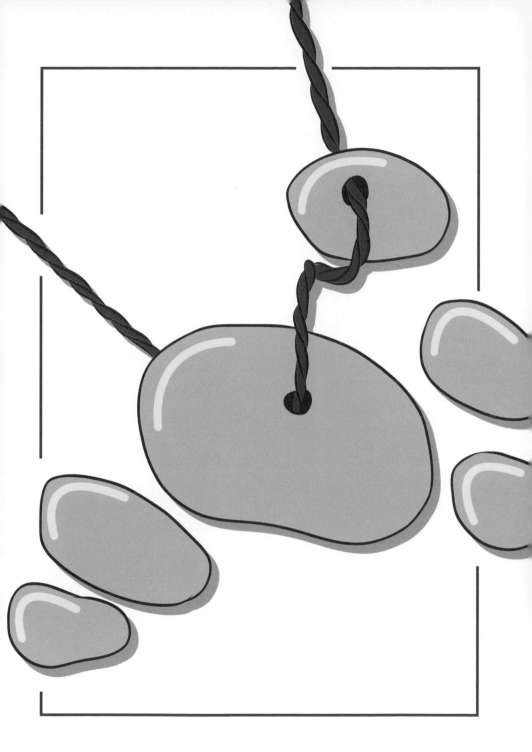

A Witch's Familiar

Familiars are animals which serve as a witch's loyal companion and sometimes assist in their magickal practice. According to folklore and legend, familiars can take any form, but as much as we might like to have a wolf or bear by our side, this would be rather impractical for the modern witch going about their day-to-day business!

Many modern witches feel a deep connection to their household pets but you do not need a cat, a hamster or even a goldfish to have a familiar. There might be a certain animal or insect that you see frequently in your garden or local park. Each of these animals has a spiritual and magickal significance and an image or likeness could be incorporated into your spell-casting for potency.

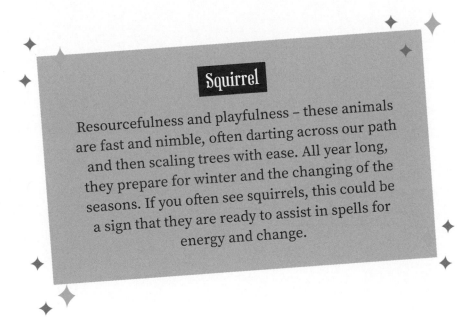

Squirrel

Resourcefulness and playfulness – these animals are fast and nimble, often darting across our path and then scaling trees with ease. All year long, they prepare for winter and the changing of the seasons. If you often see squirrels, this could be a sign that they are ready to assist in spells for energy and change.

Hedgehog

Resilience and self-knowledge – these endearing animals stand strong in their own truth. By curling up into a ball, they trust their ability to keep themselves safe and find solace in their own company. If you often see hedgehogs, this is a sign to incorporate them into spells to help you through difficult times or to help you connect to your true self.

Pigeon

Connection and freedom – pigeons are thought to be one of the first bird species to be domesticated by humans and have long been used as messengers. As such, their feathers are perfect for spells to make contact with someone from your past or simply to nurture a connection. If you often see pigeons, this could be a sign to practice magick that incorporates the element of air.

Butterfly

Transformation and new ventures – butterflies are a classic example of transformation. If you frequently see butterflies, this could be a sign that you should incorporate them into spells for growth and opportunity. This is the time to seize all opportunities that come your way, by exploring new ventures and spreading your wings.

Dragonfly

Vision and insight – these enchanting insects can see nearly a full 360 degrees and their mesmerizing eyes can also perceive colours that humans cannot. This makes them true visionaries. If you often see dragonflies, this is a sign that they are ready to assist you in your divination spells.

Bee

Strength and determination – bees have a great work ethic. They work hard but they also stop to enjoy life's nectar. If you're repeatedly seeing bees, this could be a sign that they are willing to assist in your manifestation spells so you can achieve your goals.

WITCH'S LADDER

If you're one of those people that carries around lengths of string and ribbon "just in case" your shoelace breaks, then this spell is for you because a humble piece of string can be utilized for some powerful wish magic to create a witch's ladder.

A 30 cm length will suit this type of spellcasting.

Nine days before the full moon, begin your witch's ladder by tying a knot in the string – be careful to tie the knot toward you as you visualize the fruition of your wish.

Each night, tie a new knot until the night of the full moon. Leave your witch's ladder outside to be charged by the full moon. The knots will hold the power for your wish to be realized.

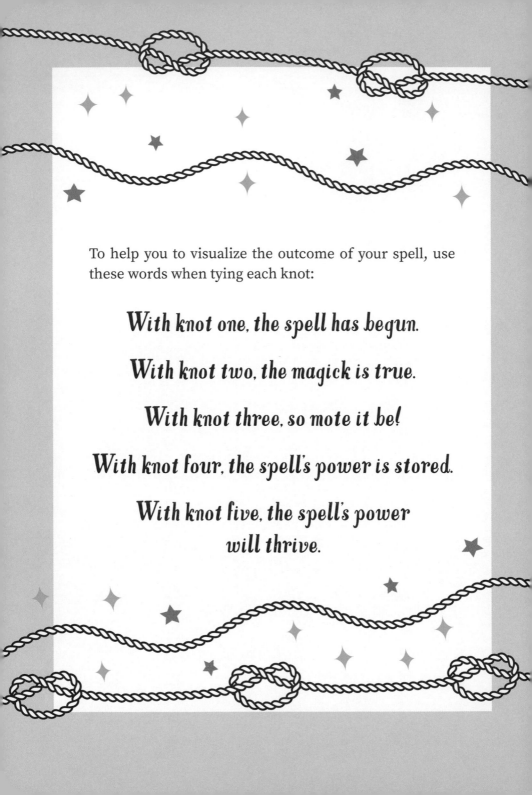

To help you to visualize the outcome of your spell, use these words when tying each knot:

With knot one, the spell has begun.

With knot two, the magick is true.

With knot three, so mote it be!

With knot four, the spell's power is stored.

With knot five, the spell's power
will thrive.

With knot six, the spell is fixed.

With knot seven, the future I leaven.

With knot eight, my spell is my fate.

With knot nine, what's done is mine.

So mote it be!

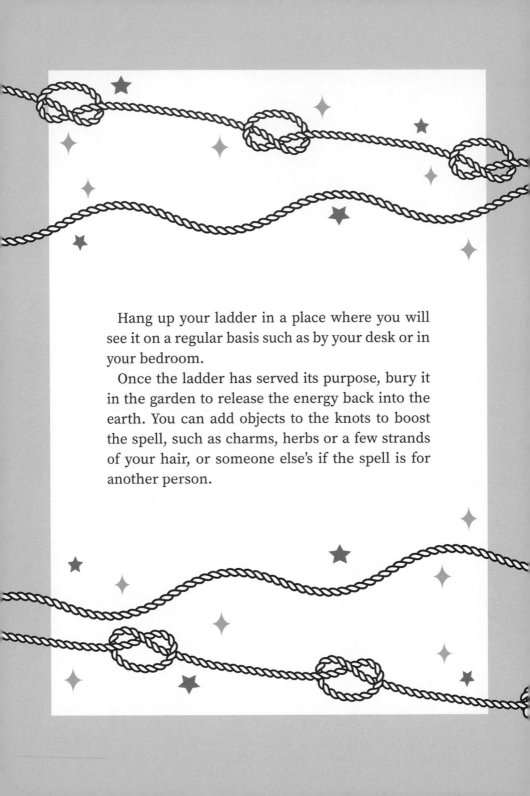

Hang up your ladder in a place where you will see it on a regular basis such as by your desk or in your bedroom.

Once the ladder has served its purpose, bury it in the garden to release the energy back into the earth. You can add objects to the knots to boost the spell, such as charms, herbs or a few strands of your hair, or someone else's if the spell is for another person.

The witch knows nothing
in this world is
supernatural.
It is all natural.

LAURIE CABOT

Chapter Five
KITCHEN WITCH

What is a kitchen witch?

The kitchen is the heart of the home and the happy place for the kitchen witch, where the worktops are their altar and the wooden spoon is their wand. Baking and cooking are rituals in themselves and when combined with herbs and spices, salt and fire, these everyday activities become the instruments for potent and powerful magick.

Tools: The kitchen witch is the herbalist, using their sense of taste and smell for manifestation. They often have a crowded windowsill of scented plants, candles and maybe even a poppet – an effigy of a past relative or deity to protect their loved ones – and the biggest selection of herbal teas you've ever seen!

MICROWAVE MAGICK

You might think you need a cauldron to be a bona fide witch. However, this is not so! The modern witch often uses the mystical magick of the microwave oven for their potions – it's clean, it's easy and those microwaves can pack a punch when they're on full power!

If you're the receiver of unwanted attention or you feel a general sense of unease, or maybe you just want to tell the world to leave you alone and let you get on with your life, here is a spell to clear away the bad vibes and unwanted visitors.

You will need

- Moon water (see page 30)
- Microwaveable dish
- Two garlic cloves – or however many external doors you have to your home
- Salt

Method

Begin by pouring the moon water into the microwaveable dish. Place the water in the microwave and heat on full power for a minute. While the water is rotating in the oven, say the following words:

Bless me!

Cleanse the bad energies around me!

So mote it be!

When the microwave has pinged, carefully remove the bowl of water and leave to stand on the kitchen worktop.

Place the garlic cloves in the water, add a pinch of salt – and throw another pinch of salt over your shoulder to get the devil in the eye!

Leave the water to cool overnight.

In the morning, take out the garlic cloves and put to one side.

Next, sprinkle the water around the entrances of your home, on the welcome mat or on the stoop while repeating the words above.

When you have finished, take the garlic cloves and push each one into a patch of earth near to the entrance of your home.

Mealtime Magick

Cooking a meal is sometimes described as an act of love and the kitchen witch is well versed in the magickal properties of edible ingredients and their powers of persuasion. Here are some common kitchen ingredients and the ways they can be used for maximum effect:

BASIL

For money and fertility

If your purse is a little emptier than you would like, wait for a waxing moon and place a few fresh basil leaves inside to draw money to you.

BAY

For enhancing psychic gifts

Cooking with bay leaves and inhaling their aroma will help you to think more clearly about the path ahead. You can also hold the leaves to the third eye – the space between your eyebrows – and think carefully about what you would like to manifest in the days and weeks ahead.

CHAMOMILE

For protection and to dispel bad dreams

Chamomile is renowned for its cleansing and calming properties. Here's a simple ritual to cleanse away bad energies and help you to sleep soundly. Switch off your phone and brew a cup of chamomile tea. While waiting for the tea to infuse, take some deep calming breaths and breathe in the aroma. Say the following words:

It's time for those bad dreams to stop

Only good things must come to me

So mote it be!

Take a sip of the tea and repeat the words after each sip.

CINNAMON

To attract money

This sweet-tasting powdered bark is delicious in desserts and has numerous magickal properties including attracting abundance, luck and love. On the eve of a new moon, place a pinch of cinnamon into your palm, open your front door and blow the cinnamon out of the house. Then say the following words:

May this cinnamon be a wish of prosperity,

good health and abundance to all who enter this house!

Sprinkle some cinnamon on your coffee when you need an extra dose of luck.

OREGANO

For happiness

An essential ingredient for spaghetti bolognese, but also widely lauded for attracting happiness. It was used by the Ancient Greeks in wedding ceremonies to ensure lasting joy. Sprinkle in a clockwise motion over your meal or around the home to encourage a sense of joy.

ROSEMARY

To enhance intuition and career success

When taken as a supplement, rosemary boosts memory and brain function, so keep this on hand as a regular flavouring for your dishes. To boost your career prospects, draw a rosemary bath by assembling some fresh rosemary stalks, tying them together with string and hanging them from your tap so the water runs over them when the bath is being filled.

For courage and emotional strength

If you have an important day coming up that requires maximum courage, such as a job interview or a driving test, make up a wish bag (a small drawstring bag) containing sprigs of fresh thyme. Get a piece of paper and write a positive affirmation to place in the bag specific to the situation, such as:

I am strong and I will shine for my job interview.

Keep the bag in a safe place, such as a handbag or purse, so you can keep it close for luck.

There are many other herbs and spices, all with different properties that can be used for spellcasting. If you want to find out more, look for a witch's herbal guide online or in bookshops.

COFFEE AND SPICE AND ALL THINGS NICE...

Coffee is an essential morning ritual for many but the kitchen witch takes their coffee ritual to the next level by adding spices for luck and prosperity. The caffeine that perks you up can energize your wishes too! This spiced coffee is ideal for wintry weather:

You will need

- Coffee – for swift results
- Ginger – to energize your ambition
- Cloves – for money luck
- Allspice – for resilience
- Cinnamon – for success and rewards
- A small dish

Method

First, make your coffee just how you like it.

Place a pinch of each of the ground spices listed above into a small dish and combine by stirring slowly in a clockwise direction. While doing this, think carefully about what you desire and imagine how you will feel when you achieve your goals.

Now sprinkle the mixed spices over your coffee and say the following words:

With this coffee and spice
I manifest my dreams
So mote it be!

Now sip your coffee and visualize the success that is coming your way.

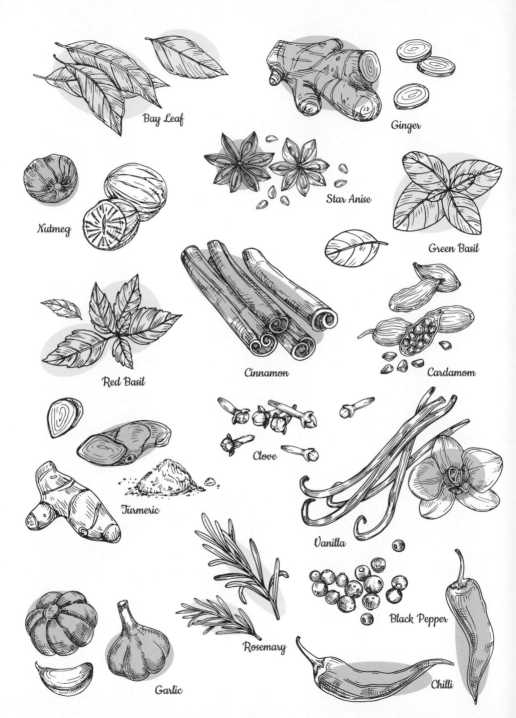

Bay Leaf

Ginger

Nutmeg

Star Anise

Green Basil

Red Basil

Cinnamon

Cardamom

Turmeric

Clove

Vanilla

Garlic

Rosemary

Black Pepper

Chilli

And for the tea drinkers...

A WISH SPELL WHILE BREWING TEA

Consider the amount of power required each time to boil a kettle – this energy can be used for quick wish spells!

You will need

- A pen and a sticky note
- A kettle
- A mug and tea bag (plus milk and sugar if you take them)

Method

Write a wish that you would like to come true on your sticky note.

Don't be greedy and ask for a million pounds because you won't get it – ask for a specific amount for something that you need, or, if you want to make a wish for someone else, add their name to the wish.

Write "So mote it be," underneath your spell. Then switch on the kettle and focus your mind on the spell, visualizing the outcome as clearly as possible.

A Spell for Good Sleep

If your mind is racing when you're trying to sleep, grab some lavender sprigs, a pinch of salt and a piece of paper (about A5 will do) and try this spell before bedtime.

You will need

- A piece of paper
- A pen or pencil to write with
- Three lavender stems
- A pinch of salt
- A piece of green string or thread
- A fireproof dish or open fire

Method

Sit quietly for a few moments on your bed and think about the things that are preventing you from a good night's sleep.

Take the piece of paper and write down three worries on it.

Next, take the lavender stems and place them in the middle of the paper. Then take the salt and sprinkle it over the lavender and the paper and say the following words:

With this lavender scent

My sleeplessness is spent

So mote it be.

Roll up the paper containing the worries, the lavender and the salt and carefully tie it with the green thread.

Leave it beside your bed as you sleep for the next three nights.

After the third night, dispose of the paper and all it contains by carefully burning it in a fireproof dish or throwing into an open fire.

A Pinch of Salt

Sometimes you just have to get salty, i.e. a little hostile, to remove an unwanted guest!

Salt is known for protection, purification and cleansing away negative vibes. If you have a possession that feels unlucky or has negative connotations, such as a ring from an ex-partner, bury it in salt and the salt will absorb and cleanse the negative energies.

If the negative energy seems to follow you, take a bath and add some Himalayan salt or sea salt to the water. Or, if you're not far from the sea, take a dip and allow the saltwater to cleanse and restore you.

If a place holds unhappy memories, sprinkle a little salt on the floor. Leave it for an hour or two to absorb the unpleasantness and then hoover it up or use a broom to sweep the salt away along with the sadness.

A Sugar Water Spell to Sweeten Them Up

Is someone in your life radiating negative energy? If you have had an argument with a friend, or if a work colleague is giving you a hard time, then this sugar water spell might well do the trick!

Just as salt repels, sugar attracts. While it may not change a person's feelings, a sugar water spell appeals to their better nature, attracting kindness and good thoughts. This will help them to recognize all your wonderful qualities and see you in a more positive light.

You will need

- A glass or bowl
- Water
- A teaspoon
- Sugar

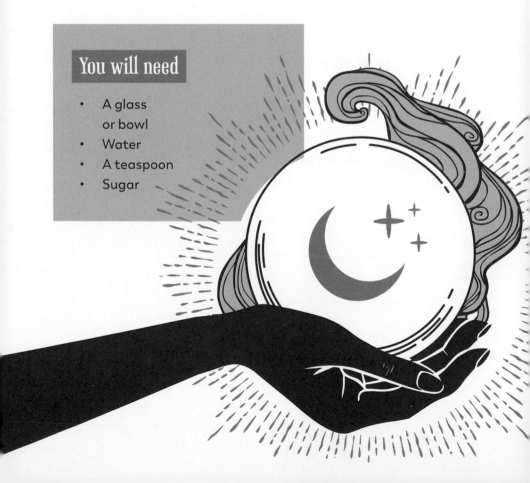

Method

Fill a glass or bowl with water. For the best results, use moon water, but tap water is fine too.

Focus on who it is that needs a little dose of sugar. Visualize them behaving positively toward you and then hold this image carefully in your mind.

Scoop up a teaspoon of sugar and add it to the water.

Speak this spell aloud:

By sugar and spice and all things nice

May sweetness last

By this spell I cast

So mote it be!

Stir clockwise until the sugar has dissolved.

The day I decided that
my life was magical,
there was suddenly
magic all around me.

MARABETH QUIN

THE
BABY WITCH'S
GRIMOIRE

It's time to cast some spells of your own

Use the following pages to record your spells or rituals and their outcomes so you can tweak and refine them for future use.

As well as trying your hand at the spells in this book, you can get creative and devise your own. It's easy and fun to do and the more you apply your own witchy instincts to a spell, the greater likelihood of success. Here are a few tips to get you started:

- First, you need to think about the premise of the spell and the goal that you are aiming for. It could be to get someone to notice you, to receive good news about a job application or even for a bit of good luck to enter your life. Think about the components required to perform the spell.

- Symbolism is very important when it comes to spellcasting. A candle is a good way of focusing your thoughts as are items that are pertinent to you and the motivation behind your spell – anything that has a special meaning to you, such as a handwritten note or a piece of jewellery. Consider the timing before you perform your spell – consider the phases of the moon (see page 23).

- Decide if you want to use the power of thought or would rather say a few words to affirm your spell. This could be a simple sentence to clarify the aim of the spell, which you repeat over and over again, or, if you're particularly good with words, you could write a rhyming couplet. Think carefully about the words before you say them – write them down as a prompt.

Once you have all of the above elements in place, you are ready to perform your spell. Make sure that you record and date your spell in your Grimoire, along with the end result.

Good luck, baby witch!

Date and time

Participants

Name of spell or ritual

Purpose

Moon phase

Ingredients and equipment

Altar

Description

Hoped-for outcome

Return to this page after one cycle of the moon and write down the results of your spell here

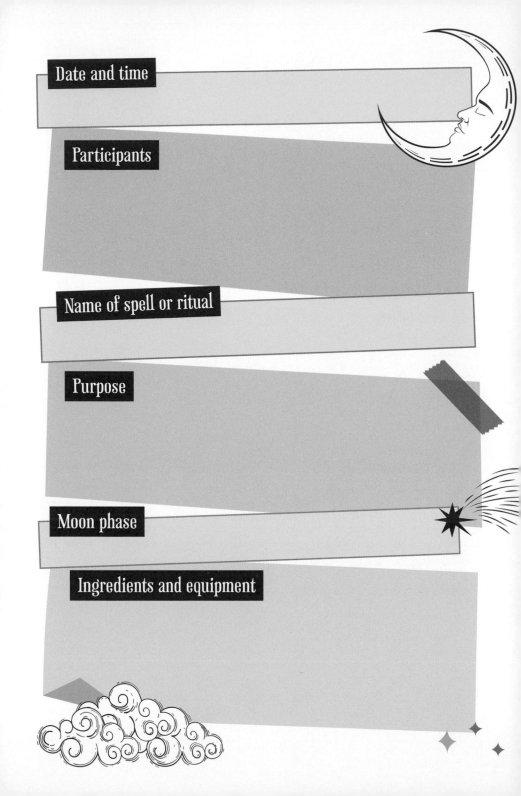

Date and time

Participants

Name of spell or ritual

Purpose

Moon phase

Ingredients and equipment

Altar

Description

Hoped-for outcome

Return to this page after one cycle of the moon and write down the results of your spell here

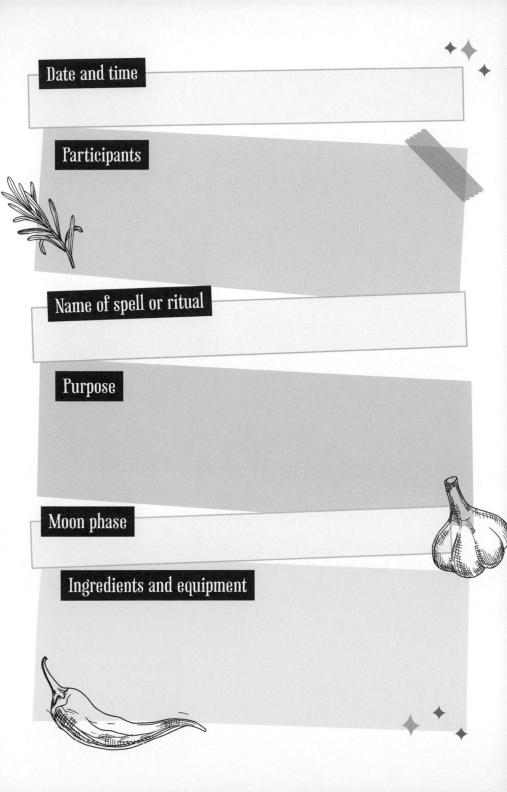

Date and time

Participants

Name of spell or ritual

Purpose

Moon phase

Ingredients and equipment

Altar

Description

Hoped-for outcome

Return to this page after one cycle of the moon and write down the results of your spell here

Date and time

Participants

Name of spell or ritual

Purpose

Moon phase

Ingredients and equipment

Altar

Description

Hoped-for outcome

Return to this page after one cycle of the moon and write down the results of your spell here

Date and time

Participants

Name of spell or ritual

Purpose

Moon phase

Ingredients and equipment

Altar

Description

Hoped-for outcome

Return to this page after one cycle of the moon and write down the results of your spell here

Date and time

Participants

Name of spell or ritual

Purpose

Moon phase

Ingredients and equipment

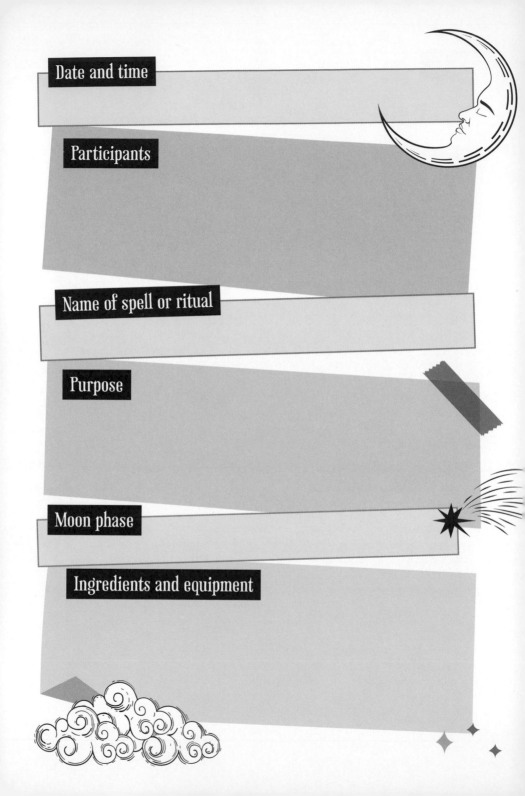

Altar

Description

Hoped-for outcome

Return to this page after one cycle of the moon and write down the results of your spell here

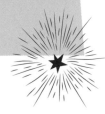

Date and time

Participants

Name of spell or ritual

Purpose

Moon phase

Ingredients and equipment

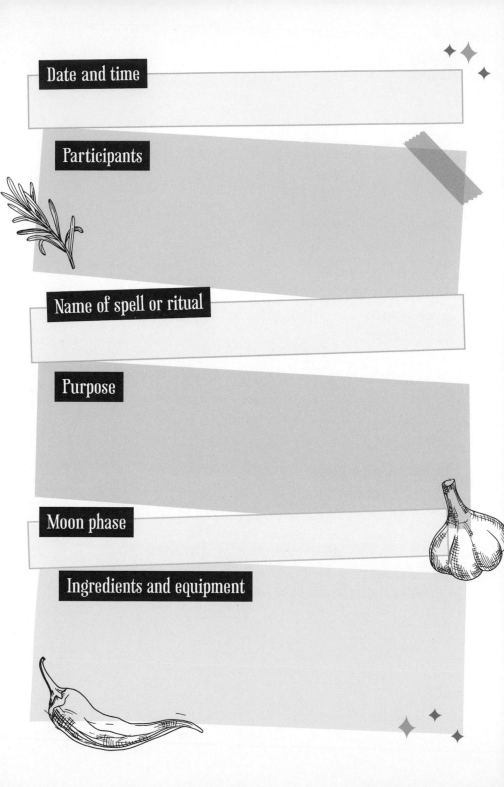

Altar

Description

Hoped-for outcome

Return to this page after one cycle of the moon and write down the results of your spell here

Date and time

Participants

Name of spell or ritual

Purpose

Moon phase

Ingredients and equipment

Altar

Description

Hoped-for outcome

Return to this page after one cycle of the moon and write down the results of your spell here

Date and time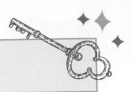

Participants

Name of spell or ritual

Purpose

Moon phase

Ingredients and equipment

Altar

Description

Hoped-for outcome

Return to this page after one cycle of the moon and write down the results of your spell here

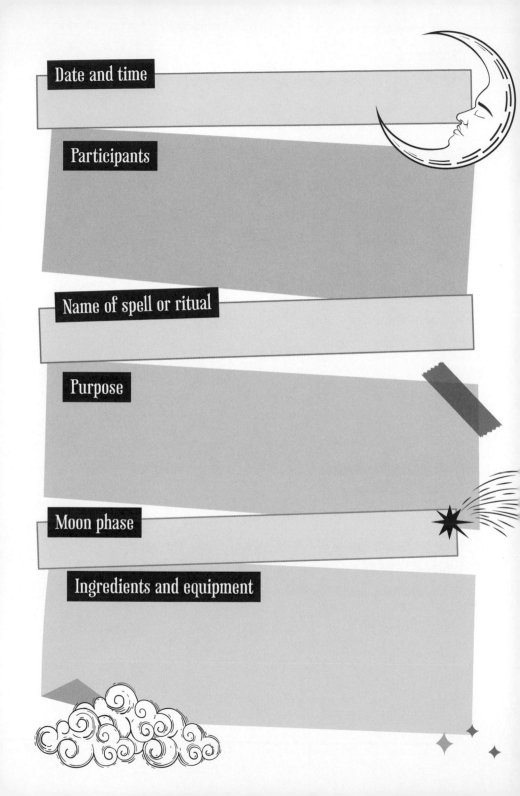

Date and time

Participants

Name of spell or ritual

Purpose

Moon phase

Ingredients and equipment

Altar

Description

Hoped-for outcome

Return to this page after one cycle of the moon and write down the results of your spell here

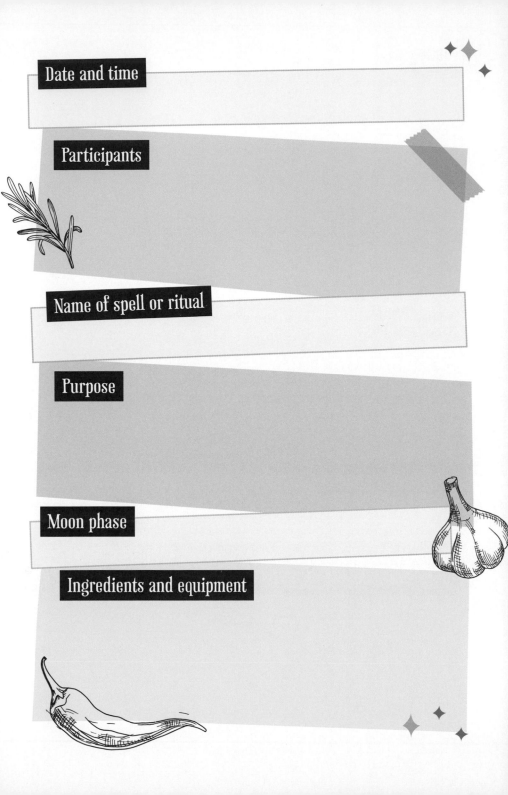

Date and time

Participants

Name of spell or ritual

Purpose

Moon phase

Ingredients and equipment

Altar

Description

Hoped-for outcome

Return to this page after one cycle of the moon and write down the results of your spell here

Date and time

Participants

Name of spell or ritual

Purpose

Moon phase

Ingredients and equipment

Altar

Description

Hoped-for outcome

Return to this page after one cycle of the moon and write down the results of your spell here

Date and time

Participants

Name of spell or ritual

Purpose

Moon phase

Ingredients and equipment

Altar

Description

Hoped-for outcome

Return to this page after one cycle of the moon and write down the results of your spell here

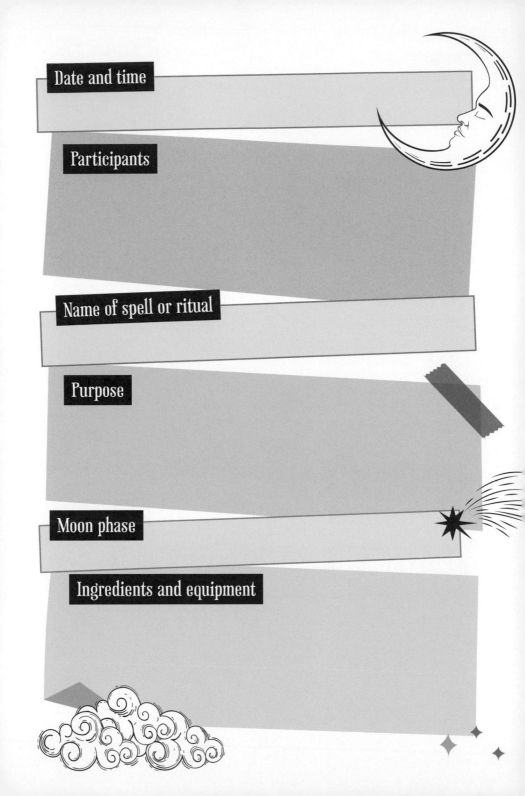

Date and time

Participants

Name of spell or ritual

Purpose

Moon phase

Ingredients and equipment

Altar

Description

Hoped-for outcome

Return to this page after one cycle of the moon and write down the results of your spell here

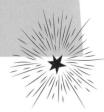

Date and time

Participants

Name of spell or ritual

Purpose

Moon phase

Ingredients and equipment

Altar

Description

Hoped-for outcome

Return to this page after one cycle of the moon and write down the results of your spell here

Date and time

Participants

Name of spell or ritual

Purpose

Moon phase

Ingredients and equipment

Altar

Description

Hoped-for outcome

Return to this page after one cycle of the moon and write down the results of your spell here

Date and time

Participants

Name of spell or ritual

Purpose

Moon phase

Ingredients and equipment

Altar

Description

Hoped-for outcome

Return to this page after one cycle of the moon and write down the results of your spell here

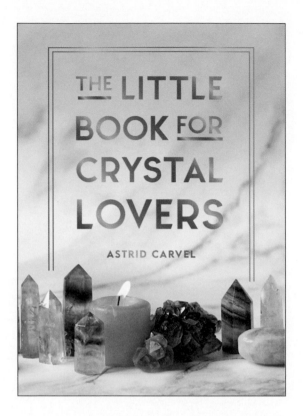

The Little Book for
Crystal Lovers

Astrid Carvel

ISBN: 978-1-80007-643-3

Harness the incredible power of crystals

Enhance your everyday life by discovering the practical and spiritual benefits of crystals. Featuring detailed profiles on dozens of stones, these pages contain everything you need to know to feel the full force of these natural treasures.

The Little Book of Tarot

Xanna Eve Chown

ISBN: 978-1-78685-798-9

Have you ever wondered what fate has in store for you?

For hundreds of years, Tarot cards have been used as a tool for divination, and a way to shed light on life's questions and challenges. With an introduction to the 78 cards and their symbols, advice on choosing your deck and tips on how to prepare and read your cards, *The Little Book of Tarot* has everything you'll need to gain your first glimpse into the misty realms of the future... what message will the cards hold for you?

Have you enjoyed this book? If so, find us
on Facebook at **Summersdale Publishers**, on
Twitter at **@Summersdale** and on Instagram and
TikTok at **@summersdalebooks** and get in touch.
We'd love to hear from you!

www.summersdale.com

Image Credits